ECUADOR TRAVEL GUIDE

Experience The Vibrant Culture And Breath-Taking Landscapes

Copyright © by Aiden C. Brooks 2024. All rights reserved.

Before this document is duplicated or reproduced in any manner, the publisher's consent must be gained. Therefore, the contents within can neither be stored electronically, transferred, nor kept in a database. Neither in Part nor full can the document be copied, scanned, faxed, or retained without approval from the publisher or creator.

TABLE OF CONTENTS

INTRODUCTION 11

Welcome to Ecuador: An Overview of the Land of Diversity 11

Why Visit Ecuador? A Journey of Culture, Nature, and Adventure..12

Quick Facts About Ecuador: Language, Currency, and Safety Tips 13

PLANNING YOUR TRIP TO ECUADOR 16

Best Time to Visit Ecuador: Climate and Seasons 16

How to Get There: Flights, Transportation, and Border Crossing Tips...17

Currency and Budgeting: How to Travel Smart in Ecuador 19

Vaccinations and Health Tips: What You Need to Know...20

Packing Essentials: Gear for Every Type of Traveler..........21

ECUADOR'S MUST-VISIT DESTINATIONS.............................23

Quito: The Capital City and Its Colonial Charm 23

Galápagos Islands: The Ultimate Wildlife Adventure........24

Cuenca: A UNESCO World Heritage City of Culture 25

Baños: Adventure Capital of Ecuador.................................26

Amazon Rainforest: Exploring the Lush Heart of Ecuador 27

Cotopaxi National Park: Hiking Ecuador's Active Volcano 28

ACTIVITIES AND EXPERIENCES 29
Adventure Activities: Hiking, Mountain Biking, and Extreme Sports 29

Beach Getaways: Surfing and Relaxing in Ecuador's Coastal Regions 31

Exploring Ecuador's Indigenous Culture and Traditions....32

Wildlife Watching: From the Amazon to the Galápagos Islands 33

Eco-Tourism: Sustainable Travel in Ecuador 34

Gastronomic Delights: What to Eat and Where to Find It.34

LOCAL CULTURE AND ETIQUETTE 36
Language: Spanish and Indigenous Languages of Ecuador36

Understanding Ecuadorian Customs and Traditions 37

What to Expect in Ecuadorian Hospitality 38

Tipping and Bargaining in Ecuador 40

SUSTAINABLE TRAVEL IN ECUADOR 41
Eco-Friendly Transportation Options in Ecuador 41

Responsible Tourism: How to Minimize Your Environmental Impact 43

Supporting Local Communities: How to Travel Responsibly 44

Volunteering and Giving Back While Traveling 45

PRACTICAL TIPS AND SAFETY 47
Travel Safety: Tips for a Smooth and Safe Experience in Ecuador 47

How to Stay Connected: Wi-Fi, SIM Cards, and Internet Access 48

Emergency Numbers and Healthcare Resources in Ecuador 50

Navigating Ecuador's Transportation System: Buses, Taxis, and Ridesharing 51

SHOPPING AND SOUVENIRS 53

Best Places to Shop for Authentic Ecuadorian Handicrafts 53

Ecuadorian Markets: What to Buy and What to Avoid 55

Eco-Friendly Souvenirs and Gifts to Bring Back Home 57

DAY TRIPS AND OFF-THE-BEATEN-PATH ADVENTURES 59

Exploring Ecuador's Hidden Gems: Secret Spots You Won't Want to Miss 59

Day Trips from Quito: Adventure, Nature, and History 61

Exploring the Quilotoa Loop: A Stunning Natural Circuit .. 62

Discovering Ecuador's Indigenous Communities: Visits and Cultural Tours 64

ECUADOR'S NIGHTLIFE AND ENTERTAINMENT 66

Quito's Best Bars, Clubs, and Live Music Venues 66

Salsa, Merengue, and Ecuadorian Dance Styles 69

Festivals and Events: Celebrating Ecuador's Rich Cultural Heritage 70

ITINERARIES FOR DIFFERENT TYPES OF TRAVELERS 73

The Classic Ecuador Itinerary: 7 Days to See the Highlights 73

Ecuador for Adventure Seekers: 10-Day Itinerary of Thrills and Nature 76

Family-Friendly Ecuador: 7 Days for All Ages 79

CONCLUSION 81

Final Thoughts on Ecuador: Why It's the Perfect Destination for Your Next Adventure 81

Additional Resources: Websites, Blogs, and Travel Forums for More Info 83

Stay Connected: How to Keep Up with Ecuadorian Travel Trends 84

APPENDICES 87

A. Useful Spanish Phrases for Travelers 87

B. Directory of Tour Operators, Travel Agencies, and Guides 89

C. Travel Resources: Websites and Apps to Make Your Trip Easier 91

D. Ecuador's Public Holidays and How They Affect Travel Plans 92

SCAN THE QR CODE

1. Open your devices camera app
2. Point the camera at the QR code
3. Ensure the code is within the frame and well-lit
4. Wait for your device to recognize the QR code
5. Once recognized, tap on the map and input your location for directions and distance

INTRODUCTION

Welcome to Ecuador: An Overview of the Land of Diversity

Imagine stepping into a place where the sky seems endless, the mountains stretch like ancient guardians, and the air is fragrant with the rich scents of lush rainforests and salty sea breezes. Welcome to Ecuador, a tiny country on the equator that is packed to the brim with stunning landscapes, vibrant cultures, and an adventure waiting around every corner.

Ecuador may be small in size, but it's massive in what it offers. From the soaring peaks of the Andes to the untouched wilderness of the Amazon rainforest, from colonial cities like Quito, with their cobblestone streets and historical charm, to the remote Galápagos Islands, where wildlife thrives in its purest form, Ecuador is a land of diversity—both in landscapes and in people. Whether you're an adrenaline junkie, a nature lover, a history buff, or a beachgoer, Ecuador has something uniquely memorable to offer. The country's compact size means that in just a few hours, you can travel from one world to the next—from the misty mountain towns to the sun-kissed coastal villages.

As someone who's called Ecuador home for many years, let me tell you —it's not just a destination; it's a journey into a world where every experience is as diverse as the country itself. Ecuador feels like a warm embrace—its people are welcoming, its landscapes jaw-dropping, and its pace of life feels like an invitation to relax, explore, and lose yourself in the beauty of it all.

Why Visit Ecuador? A Journey of Culture, Nature, and Adventure

Ecuador is a country that wears its heart on its sleeve, brimming with a passionate culture that connects every corner of the land. The culture here is deeply rooted in history—Indigenous traditions coexist with Spanish colonial influences to create a beautiful, sometimes unexpected fusion. The people are proud of their heritage, and you'll experience this in their music, dance, cuisine, and festivals, which paint Ecuador's vibrant cultural canvas.

Let's start with Ecuador's natural beauty. Imagine hiking in the Andean mountains, where snow-capped volcanoes rise above you and lush valleys teeming with exotic wildlife lie below. Whether you're looking for a challenge or just a peaceful hike, the trails here will steal your breath away. Then there's the Amazon basin—the lungs of the Earth, a world where the air smells of wet earth, and every tree and leaf hums with life. It's a paradise for birdwatchers and nature lovers, where the world's most incredible biodiversity exists in a balance of natural perfection.

And we can't forget the Galápagos Islands, a place like no other on Earth. The very word "Galápagos" conjures images of giant tortoises, blue-footed boobies, and volcanic landscapes that feel as though they belong on another planet. This archipelago, a UNESCO World Heritage Site, offers one of the most unique wildlife experiences on the planet. Here, the animals have no fear of humans, offering close-up encounters that are simply awe-inspiring.

Adventure seekers will find their heart's content in Ecuador. Whether it's surfing in the Pacific, rafting through the wild rivers of the Amazon, paragliding over the valleys of Baños, or climbing to the summit of an active volcano, Ecuador will get your pulse racing in the best way. There is no shortage of thrilling experiences here, each one set against an extraordinarily beautiful backdrop.

Quick Facts About Ecuador: Language, Currency, and Safety Tips

When you land in Ecuador, one of the first things you'll notice is that the people are incredibly warm and eager to share their country with visitors. Spanish is the official language here, but many Indigenous languages like Quichua and Shuar are also spoken in certain regions, particularly in the Amazon and the highlands. It's helpful (but not essential) to learn a few basic Spanish phrases like *hola* (hello), *gracias* (thank you), and *¿cuánto cuesta?* (how much does it cost?) to show respect for the culture. You'll find that many people in the major cities and tourist spots speak some English, but in more remote areas, speaking Spanish will help you connect with locals.

Ecuador's currency is the U.S. dollar, which is a huge convenience for American travelers. You won't need to worry about currency exchange rates, as the U.S. dollar is accepted everywhere—from the bustling markets of Quito to the remote villages of the Amazon. ATMs are widely available in cities, and credit cards are accepted at most hotels, restaurants, and larger shops, though it's always a good idea to carry cash for smaller purchases or in more rural areas.

Safety-wise, Ecuador is generally a safe country to travel to, though like in any other destination, it's wise to take common-sense precautions. Petty theft, such as pickpocketing, can happen in busy areas, so always keep an eye on your belongings, especially in crowded markets or public transportation. The major cities, including Quito and Guayaquil, have certain neighborhoods that are best avoided at night, but with proper precautions, you'll find Ecuador to be a safe and friendly destination. Emergency numbers to keep handy: Police (101), Medical Emergencies (131), and Fire Department (102).

Contact Information & Useful Numbers

- **Tourism Office in Quito**: Ministry of Tourism of Ecuador
    - Address: Cordero N24-338, Quito, Ecuador
    - Phone: +593 2-250-3533
    - Website: www.turismo.gob.ec
- **Galápagos Islands National Park**:

- - Phone: +593 5-252-6175
  - Website: www.galapagos.org
- **Quito International Airport** (Mariscal Sucre International Airport):
  - Address: Av. de los Shyris y Av. Amazonas, Quito, Ecuador
  - Phone: +593 2-294-5000
  - Website: www.aeropuertoquito.aero
- **Emergency Numbers**:
  - Police: 101
  - Fire Department: 102
  - Medical Emergencies: 131

As for accommodations, you'll find options for all budgets across Ecuador, from luxurious resorts in the Andes to eco-lodges nestled in the Amazon. A few spots to consider are:

- **Casa Gangotena** (Quito): A luxury boutique hotel set in a restored colonial mansion in the heart of Old Quito.
  - Address: Calle Bolívar Oe6-41, Quito, Ecuador
  - Phone: +593 2-256-2262
- **Mashpi Lodge** (Cloud Forest): A premium eco-lodge surrounded by pristine forest in the Andean foothills.
  - Address: Pacto, Ecuador
  - Phone: +593 2-382-0851

PLANNING YOUR TRIP TO ECUADOR

Best Time to Visit Ecuador: Climate and Seasons

Ecuador is a country where the seasons don't follow the usual patterns. Thanks to its position along the equator, Ecuador has a relatively mild and diverse climate throughout the year. But that doesn't mean there isn't a "best" time to visit—it's just that the best time depends on what kind of experience you're looking for.

The beauty of Ecuador lies in its microclimates. You can be standing in the warmth of a beach town one moment, then find yourself at a high-altitude Andean market in a sweater the next. The highlands, where cities like Quito and Cuenca sit, enjoy a temperate climate year-round. Days are often sunny and cool, and nights can get chilly, especially in the mountains. Meanwhile, the coast offers a tropical climate with humidity and heat, and the Amazon jungle is hot, humid, and rainy, no matter the time of year.

When it comes to planning your trip, the most important factor is the rainy season. From December to May, the weather in the coastal and Amazonian regions can be unpredictable, with frequent afternoon showers that transform the landscape into a lush, vibrant green. The rainy season in the highlands is less intense but still worth considering, especially if you plan on hiking volcanoes or exploring remote areas.

The dry season, from June to September, is typically considered the best time to visit, especially for outdoor adventures. The skies are clearer, perfect for trekking the Andes or exploring the Galápagos Islands. However, this period can also be more crowded, especially in popular tourist areas, so it's a good idea to plan and book in advance.

If your trip centers around the Galápagos, keep in mind that the best time to visit depends on your interests. For warmer waters and more active wildlife, plan a visit between December and May. If you're after cooler waters and less crowded conditions, June through November is ideal.

How to Get There: Flights, Transportation, and Border Crossing Tips

Getting to Ecuador is easier than you might think, thanks to its well-connected international airports. Most travelers fly into *Mariscal Sucre International Airport* in Quito (UIO) or *José Joaquín de Olmedo International Airport* in Guayaquil (GYE), with Quito serving as the main gateway to the highlands, and Guayaquil as the key hub for those heading to the coast.

Flights from the U.S. to Ecuador typically take around 4-5 hours from Miami or New York, making it an accessible destination from North America. Major international airlines like American Airlines, Delta, and Avianca, as well as low-cost carriers, offer regular flights to Quito and Guayaquil. From Europe, expect a flight time of about 12-14 hours, with most flights connecting through Madrid, Amsterdam, or Bogotá.

Once you've arrived, getting around Ecuador is relatively straightforward. The bus system is reliable and affordable, connecting major cities like Quito, Cuenca, and Guayaquil, as well as smaller towns throughout the country. For shorter trips or more direct routes, flights are also available with domestic carriers like *TAME* or *Avianca*, and there are plenty of taxis, rental cars, and ride-hailing apps like Uber in the larger cities.

For those planning to visit the Galápagos Islands, flights depart from Quito or Guayaquil. The two main airports on the islands are *Seymour Airport* on Baltra Island and *San Cristóbal Airport* on San Cristóbal Island, both of which are served by daily flights. It's important to note that visitors to the Galápagos need a special transit control card, which can be purchased at the airport for $20 USD.

If you're crossing borders from neighboring countries, Ecuador's land borders with Colombia and Peru are easy to navigate. The *Rumichaca* border with Colombia, near Tulcán, is the busiest, while the *Aguas Verdes* border with Peru is well-served by buses and taxis. Remember that Ecuador is part of the Andean Community, so traveling within South America is straightforward. Ensure you have the necessary visa if required, and check for any updates or requirements on vaccinations or border restrictions.

Currency and Budgeting: How to Travel Smart in Ecuador

Ecuador uses the U.S. Dollar (USD) as its official currency, which makes it very convenient for American travelers. You won't need to worry about currency exchange, which is a big plus. Banknotes are in the same denominations as U.S. currency, and you'll find coins, but they are local Ecuadorian *centavos* (similar to U.S. pennies and nickels).

Ecuador is an affordable destination for travelers on a budget. Accommodation prices can vary depending on where you stay, but you'll find a range of options. Budget travelers can find dormitories and simple guesthouses for as little as $10-$20 USD per night, while mid-range hotels can range from $30 to $100 USD. Upscale resorts, especially in places like the Galápagos or luxury lodges in the Amazon, can cost upwards of $200 USD per night.

Food in Ecuador is inexpensive. Street food like empanadas, arepas, or *ceviche* (especially on the coast) is delicious and typically costs just a few dollars. A sit-down meal at a local restaurant may range from $5-$15 USD, and a three-course meal at a higher-end restaurant can run you about $25-$40 USD.

For transportation, Ecuador has affordable buses, which will cost you just a couple of dollars to travel between cities. If you're traveling within Quito or Guayaquil, taxis are reasonably priced, with fares starting around $1.50 USD. For those looking to rent a car, daily rates can start from $25 USD per day, excluding insurance.

ATMs are widely available in cities, and credit cards are accepted in most larger establishments. However, always have cash on hand for smaller purchases in remote areas or markets.

Vaccinations and Health Tips: What You Need to Know

Ecuador is generally a safe place to travel in terms of health, but it's always wise to take a few precautions before you go. For starters, make sure you're up to date on routine vaccines like measles, mumps, rubella (MMR), tetanus, and hepatitis A and B. The CDC recommends that travelers to Ecuador also consider getting vaccines for typhoid, yellow fever, and rabies, especially if you plan to visit the Amazon or travel to rural areas.

Yellow fever vaccination is required if you're traveling to the Amazon region, as well as certain parts of the coast. You'll need proof of vaccination if you're traveling to these areas. Also, carry insect repellent to avoid mosquito-borne illnesses such as dengue, Zika, and malaria, especially in tropical and lowland areas.

Tap water in Ecuador isn't always safe to drink, especially in rural or jungle regions, so it's advisable to buy bottled water or carry a water filter for outdoor activities. If you're trekking or heading into remote areas, make sure you're well-prepared with snacks, water, and first-aid essentials.

It's also a good idea to pack a small medical kit with basic over-the-counter medications, especially if you're planning on hiking or engaging in outdoor activities. Many pharmacies are available in urban areas, and they offer a range of medicines if needed, but it's always better to be prepared.

Packing Essentials: Gear for Every Type of Traveler

What you pack for Ecuador will depend largely on where you're going and what activities you plan to do. For the highlands, bring layers—daytime temperatures are mild, but evenings can get cold. A light jacket, warm fleece, and comfortable walking shoes are key. For trekking in the mountains or volcanoes, sturdy hiking boots and a backpack with rain cover are essential.

If you're visiting the Amazon, light, breathable clothing is a must. Long sleeves and pants will protect you from mosquitoes, and a good pair of waterproof boots is a necessity for jungle trekking. Don't forget insect repellent, sunscreen, and a wide-brimmed hat for sun protection.

For those heading to the coast, lightweight clothing is your best friend, but make sure to pack a good swimsuit, sunglasses, and sunscreen for the sunny days ahead. A beach bag, along with sandals and a waterproof camera, will serve you well.

No matter where you're traveling in Ecuador, always carry a small first-aid kit, a reusable water bottle, and, of course, your camera to capture the beautiful landscapes. Whether you're hiking the Andes, exploring the Amazon, or lounging on the beach, your trip to Ecuador will be an unforgettable adventure.

Contact Information & Useful Numbers

- **Quito International Airport (Mariscal Sucre International Airport)**
  Address: Av. de los Shyris y Av. Amazonas, Quito, Ecuador
  Phone: +593 2-294-5000
  Website: www.aeropuertoquito.aero
- **Galápagos National Park**
  Phone: +593 5-252-6175
  Website: www.galapagos.org
- **Tourism Ministry of Ecuador**
  Address: Cordero N24-338, Quito, Ecuador
  Phone: +593 2-250-3533
  Website: www.turismo.gob.ec

ECUADOR'S MUST-VISIT DESTINATIONS

Quito: The Capital City and Its Colonial Charm

Nestled high in the Andes at over 9,000 feet above sea level, Quito, Ecuador's capital, is one of the most captivating cities in South America. It's a place where history is alive on every corner, and the crisp mountain air mixes with the aroma of freshly brewed coffee. When you arrive in Quito, you'll immediately feel its unique blend of old-world charm and modernity, a city whose colonial heart beats strong in the face of modern development.

Quito's *Centro Histórico* (historic center) is the star of the show. With its narrow cobblestone streets, ornate churches, and charming squares, the area is a living testament to Ecuador's colonial past. The UNESCO World Heritage-listed Old Town is a labyrinth of stunning architecture, including the *Iglesia de la Compañía de Jesús*, a church renowned for its baroque architecture and gilded interiors that will leave you speechless. Spend an afternoon wandering around *Plaza Grande*, the main square, where you can marvel at the presidential palace and the imposing *Catedral Metropolitana*. As you stroll, the city's vibrant mix of colonial-era buildings and colorful modern murals is a constant reminder that Quito is a city of contrasts.

Beyond the historical beauty, Quito offers a wide range of experiences. You can take a cable car up *Pichincha Volcano* for panoramic views of the city or hike to the summit for an unforgettable sunrise. If you're after something a bit more modern, the *La Ronda* neighborhood is a great spot for vibrant street art, artisan shops, and a taste of Ecuadorian nightlife.

For those interested in nature, Quito's proximity to the *Mitad del Mundo* (Middle of the World) monument offers a chance to stand on the equator, where you can straddle both hemispheres—an iconic photo opportunity.

Galápagos Islands: The Ultimate Wildlife Adventure

A trip to Ecuador wouldn't be complete without visiting the *Galápagos Islands*, a paradise for nature lovers and wildlife enthusiasts. Located around 600 miles off the coast, this archipelago is home to some of the most diverse and unique species on the planet, many of which can only be found here. The Galápagos are a living laboratory of evolution, famously studied by Charles Darwin, and they remain one of the world's most extraordinary destinations for wildlife.

The islands' volcanic landscape is striking—imagine dramatic cliffs, sandy beaches, and crystal-clear waters teeming with marine life. Spend your days snorkeling with sea lions, swimming alongside giant manta rays, or observing the famous *Galápagos tortoises* in their natural habitat. The islands are a birdwatcher's dream as well, with unique species like the *blue-footed booby* and the *Galápagos finch* putting on quite a show.

Most visitors arrive by air, flying from Quito or Guayaquil to *Baltra Island* or *San Cristóbal Island*, both of which have well-connected airports. The islands are also home to a variety of eco-lodges and boat cruises, each offering a unique way to experience the Galápagos' pristine beauty. Whether you're on a guided tour of *Santa Cruz Island* or hiking to the rim of *Sierra Negra Volcano* on *Isabela Island*, the Galápagos will leave you with memories that last a lifetime.

Cuenca: A UNESCO World Heritage City of Culture

Cuenca, often considered Ecuador's most picturesque city, is a UNESCO World Heritage gem that invites you to slow down and savor the beauty of its cobbled streets and colonial architecture. Tucked into the Andean highlands, Cuenca is a place where art, culture, and tradition blend seamlessly. Walking through the city feels like stepping back in time—its stunning *cathedrals*, colorful markets, and boutique shops add to the city's charming allure.

Start your journey in the *Plaza Calderón*, Cuenca's central square, where you'll find the magnificent *Catedral Nueva* with its striking blue-domed roof. The square is lined with cafes and artisan shops, making it the perfect spot to relax and people-watch. Don't miss the *Museo Pumapungo*, a fascinating museum that explores the area's pre-Columbian history, or the *Tomebamba River*, which flows through the heart of the city and offers scenic walking paths.

Cuenca is also a fantastic place to experience Ecuadorian craftsmanship, particularly the famous *Panama hats*. Despite their name, Panama hats actually hail from Ecuador, and you'll find plenty of artisans crafting these fine hats by hand. Cuenca's vibrant art scene is alive with galleries and local exhibitions, making it a haven for those looking to immerse themselves in Ecuadorian culture.

Baños: Adventure Capital of Ecuador

Nestled between the towering Andes and the lush Amazon basin, *Baños* is known as the adventure capital of Ecuador, and for good reason. If you're someone who thrives on adrenaline, this is the place for you. Baños is famous for its waterfalls—over 60 of them cascade down the surrounding mountains—and you can visit many of them by foot, bike, or even horseback. *Pailón del Diablo*, or the "Devil's Cauldron," is the most famous, where you can hike through the forest and feel the mist from the powerful waterfall as it crashes into the river below.

But Baños isn't just about waterfalls; it's an outdoor enthusiast's playground. You can go canyoning, paragliding, rafting, or take a cable car ride across the *Rio Pastaza* valley, which offers breathtaking views of the landscape below. The town itself is charming, with a mix of Ecuadorian culture and adventure tourism. In the evenings, unwind in one of the hot springs after a day of adventure, and soak in the healing waters while surrounded by stunning mountain views.

Baños also offers a wealth of hiking trails, including a trek to the *Tungurahua Volcano*, which has been active since 1999. While the volcano is unpredictable, hiking around the base offers a chance to observe the surrounding ecosystems and get close to the indigenous flora and fauna.

Amazon Rainforest: Exploring the Lush Heart of Ecuador

For those seeking an unforgettable adventure deep in the heart of nature, the *Amazon Rainforest* is one of Ecuador's most awe-inspiring destinations. Covering more than 50% of the country's territory, the Amazon basin is a vast expanse of tropical jungle, home to thousands of species of animals, plants, and insects.

A visit to the Amazon offers a true sense of wilderness and adventure. Guided tours often start in *Tena*, a small city on the edge of the rainforest, where you can embark on boat trips down the *Napo River* to reach eco-lodges hidden deep in the jungle. From there, you'll explore trails that wind through the forest, taking in the sounds of birds, monkeys, and the rustling of leaves. You can go canoeing on tranquil rivers, birdwatching, or even visit local *Shuar* or *Kichwa* indigenous communities to learn about their traditions and way of life.

The Amazon is also an opportunity to experience the incredible biodiversity of Ecuador's tropical ecosystems. While trekking, you might spot *poison dart frogs*, *anacondas*, and colorful *macaws*, and even discover medicinal plants used by local communities for centuries.

Cotopaxi National Park: Hiking Ecuador's Active Volcano

Ecuador is home to some of the most stunning natural landscapes in South America, and *Cotopaxi National Park* is a true highlight for hikers and adventure seekers. Located just 30 miles south of Quito, *Cotopaxi* is one of the highest active volcanoes in the world, standing at 19,347 feet tall. Its nearly perfect symmetrical cone rises dramatically above the Andean plains, making it one of the most iconic mountains in Ecuador.

For those who are up for the challenge, hiking Cotopaxi is an experience like no other. While it's possible to trek to the summit, most visitors opt to hike to the *José F. Rivas* refuge at 15,744 feet, which offers panoramic views of the surrounding highlands and glaciers. For those who aren't keen on a strenuous trek, the park's lower altitudes provide stunning landscapes, with wildlife such as wild horses and Andean condors flying overhead.

Cotopaxi National Park is also a fantastic place to explore on horseback or mountain bike, with several scenic trails that offer breathtaking views of the volcano and the surrounding páramo ecosystem.

ACTIVITIES AND EXPERIENCES

Ecuador is a country that thrives on its diversity—from the towering peaks of the Andes to the lush Amazon rainforest and the pristine shores of the Pacific. Whether you're an adrenaline junkie, a culture seeker, or someone who just wants to sit back and savor the moment, Ecuador offers a wealth of activities that cater to every kind of traveler. In this chapter, we'll dive into the activities that will make your visit unforgettable, from extreme sports to cultural exploration and delicious culinary experiences.

Adventure Activities: Hiking, Mountain Biking, and Extreme Sports

For those whose hearts beat faster when faced with a challenge, Ecuador is a playground of outdoor adventure. The dramatic geography of this small country makes it one of the best destinations in the world for hiking, mountain biking, and extreme sports. The towering peaks of the Andes provide endless opportunities for adventure, while the valleys and mountains offer routes for all levels of explorers.

One of the most famous hikes is the trek to the summit of *Cotopaxi*, one of the highest active volcanoes in the world. While summiting Cotopaxi requires a high level of fitness and preparation, a simpler yet equally rewarding option is the hike to the *José F. Rivas* refuge. At over 15,000 feet, the views of the surrounding glaciers, volcanic landscapes, and the Pacific coast are absolutely jaw-dropping. Hiking this route offers not only an incredible workout but an insight into the Andean wilderness and the breathtaking beauty of the area.

For something less intense but equally stunning, consider hiking through the lush *Cajas National Park*, located just outside of Cuenca. The park features 232 lagoons, mountain trails, and dramatic landscapes, offering a unique combination of high-altitude hiking and cloud forest experiences.

Mountain biking is another exhilarating way to experience Ecuador's landscape. From the high-altitude roads of the Andes to the rugged paths that descend into the Amazon basin, the country has a range of routes that will satisfy even the most experienced bikers. One of the most popular routes is the *Chimborazo* descent, where you'll cycle down from the summit of Ecuador's highest peak, an exhilarating journey with views that will take your breath away.

If extreme sports are your thing, Ecuador will not disappoint. You can experience the thrill of *canyoning* (waterfall rappelling) in the lush, rugged landscapes around *Baños*, where waterfalls cascade down cliffs in spectacular displays. The adrenaline rush of paragliding over the *Andes* or the *Cotopaxi* volcano is a bucket-list experience for many, giving you a bird's eye view of the land below. Ecuador's diverse terrain is tailor-made for those seeking thrills in the great outdoors.

Beach Getaways: Surfing and Relaxing in Ecuador's Coastal Regions

Ecuador's Pacific coast offers a stunning blend of surf spots, laid-back beach towns, and rich marine life. Whether you're a seasoned surfer or someone just looking to soak up the sun, the country's coastal regions have something special to offer.

Montañita is perhaps the most famous beach town in Ecuador, known for its world-class waves, vibrant nightlife, and laid-back bohemian vibe. Whether you're catching waves or sipping on a cold *pina colada* while watching the sunset, Montañita is a must-visit for beach lovers. The surf here caters to all levels, from beginners to experts, and there are plenty of surf schools for those looking to catch their first wave.

If you're looking for something quieter and more off the beaten path, head to *Canoa*, a sleepy beach town north of *Montañita*. Canoa offers long stretches of golden sand, perfect for those who enjoy a more peaceful beach experience. It's ideal for relaxing, swimming, or enjoying fresh seafood right on the beach. Further north, the *Machalilla National Park* offers pristine beaches like *Los Frailes*, where the stunning cliffs meet crystal-clear waters.

For those looking to combine surfing with wildlife watching, *Salinas* is a great spot. Known as the "Ecuadorian Riviera," Salinas is home to an array of marine life and offers some of the best conditions for both surfing and kitesurfing in the country.

Exploring Ecuador's Indigenous Culture and Traditions

Ecuador's indigenous culture is an integral part of the country's identity, and there is no better way to connect with the country's deep roots than by exploring its indigenous communities. Throughout the country, indigenous groups like the *Kichwa*, *Shuar*, and *Otavalo* maintain rich cultural traditions that are woven into the daily fabric of life.

One of the most famous and accessible ways to experience indigenous culture is by visiting the *Otavalo Market*, located in the highland town of Otavalo. The market, which is one of the largest in South America, is a kaleidoscope of color, with artisans selling everything from vibrant textiles and handcrafted jewelry to leather goods and pottery. This bustling market is a great place to learn about the Andean way of life, and you can chat with local artisans about their craft while picking up some beautiful souvenirs.

Further into the Amazon basin, you can visit the *Kichwa* and *Shuar* communities, where you'll have the chance to learn about traditional crafts, medicinal plants, and the spiritual practices that have been passed down for generations. Some communities offer tours where you can participate in cooking workshops, visit local healers, and gain a deeper understanding of the indigenous worldview.

In the highlands, traditional festivals like *Inti Raymi* in *June* offer visitors an incredible chance to experience Ecuador's indigenous culture through music, dance, and ritual. The festival celebrates the Inca sun god and is a beautiful blend of Andean spirituality and community celebration.

Wildlife Watching: From the Amazon to the Galápagos Islands

Ecuador is a paradise for wildlife lovers, offering some of the most diverse and accessible wildlife experiences in the world. The country's ecosystems—from the Amazon rainforest to the Galápagos Islands—are home to a wealth of creatures that are both fascinating and unique.

In the Amazon, you can embark on a riverboat tour along the *Napo River*, spotting monkeys, sloths, and colorful birds. The rainforests of Ecuador are teeming with life, and a guided tour with an experienced naturalist is one of the best ways to observe the incredible biodiversity. Be sure to keep an eye out for the elusive jaguar and the infamous *poison dart frogs*.

But Ecuador's wildlife watching crown jewel is undoubtedly the *Galápagos Islands*. The islands are a living museum of evolution, where you can interact with wildlife that's found nowhere else on Earth. From swimming with sea lions to observing the famous giant tortoises, the Galápagos is a once-in-a-lifetime destination for nature lovers. Every island has its own character, offering visitors the chance to spot everything from marine iguanas basking on the rocks to the colorful *blue-footed boobies* performing their courtship dance.

Eco-Tourism: Sustainable Travel in Ecuador

As one of the world's most biodiverse countries, Ecuador is also leading the charge in eco-tourism, encouraging travelers to explore the country responsibly and sustainably. Whether you're hiking in the cloud forests of the Andes or cruising through the Galápagos, there are plenty of opportunities to minimize your environmental impact.

Eco-lodges are a great way to stay in harmony with nature while supporting local communities. In the Amazon, many lodges are run by indigenous communities and practice sustainable tourism, offering guests the chance to learn about traditional ecological practices and the importance of conservation.

In the Galápagos, tour operators and accommodations are working hard to maintain the integrity of the islands' ecosystems. Responsible tourism here includes following strict rules to protect wildlife, minimizing plastic use, and supporting local conservation efforts.

Gastronomic Delights: What to Eat and Where to Find It

Ecuadorian cuisine is a feast for the senses, and the country's diversity is reflected in its food. From the coastal regions to the highlands and the Amazon, each area has its own unique flavors and dishes to discover.

Start with the famous *ceviche*, which can be found in coastal towns like *Guayaquil* and *Montañita*. The freshest fish is marinated in citrus and mixed with onions, cilantro, and a bit of heat from chili peppers—perfect for a warm afternoon by the sea. Another coastal favorite is *encebollado*, a hearty fish soup that's often enjoyed for breakfast, accompanied by a side of rice or plantains.

In the highlands, you'll find heartier fare like *locro de papa*, a potato soup made with creamy cheese and served with avocado, or *hornado*, slow-roasted pork served with crispy skin and a side of *mote* (hominy). And let's not forget *empanadas*, which are stuffed with cheese or meat and make for a perfect snack.

One of the most unique culinary experiences in Ecuador is a visit to a traditional *pachamanca* feast, where meat and vegetables are cooked in an underground oven. Often part of indigenous ceremonies or celebrations, this is an experience that will immerse you in Ecuador's rich culinary traditions.

From street food stalls to high-end restaurants, Ecuador's food scene will undoubtedly leave you wanting more. Don't forget to try *chicha*, a traditional fermented drink made from maize, or sip on some local *canelazo*, a warm spiced drink made with sugarcane alcohol, cinnamon, and cloves—perfect for chilly Andean evenings.

LOCAL CULTURE AND ETIQUETTE

Ecuador is a country rich in cultural diversity, where indigenous heritage, colonial history, and modern influences intertwine seamlessly. From the highland towns where Andean traditions still flourish, to the bustling markets and beachside villages, the local culture in Ecuador is as colorful and diverse as its landscapes. Understanding the intricacies of Ecuadorian customs, language, and hospitality will enhance your travels and allow you to connect with the locals in meaningful ways. This chapter will take you through the essential cultural aspects, from the language spoken to the etiquettes you should keep in mind when interacting with the Ecuadorian people.

Language: Spanish and Indigenous Languages of Ecuador

Spanish is the official language of Ecuador, and it's the language you'll hear in most places, from the cities to the countryside. However, Ecuador's linguistic landscape is far more diverse. The country is home to a variety of indigenous groups, many of which speak their own languages. The most widely spoken indigenous languages include *Quechua, Shuar,* and *Kichwa*.

In the Andean highlands, *Kichwa* is widely spoken, especially in towns like Otavalo, where the indigenous Otavaleños use it to communicate in daily life. In the Amazon basin, the *Shuar* people speak their native tongue, while *Quechua* is spoken by various communities across the central and southern highlands, including the famous city of Cuenca. While most Ecuadorians will understand and speak Spanish fluently, there's something special about hearing an indigenous language spoken with pride.

If you're planning to visit rural areas or indigenous villages, learning a few basic Spanish phrases will go a long way. Simple greetings like *"Buenos días"* (Good morning) and *"Gracias"* (Thank you) will endear you to the locals. In certain regions, such as the Amazon, greeting the local people in their indigenous language, or even showing curiosity about their cultural heritage, can be a meaningful gesture that will be warmly appreciated.

Understanding Ecuadorian Customs and Traditions

Ecuador is a country where tradition is deeply embedded in everyday life, and its festivals, rituals, and customs are an essential part of its national identity. A trip to Ecuador is as much about experiencing its vibrant culture as it is about exploring its natural beauty.

The *Inti Raymi*, or Festival of the Sun, is one of the most important celebrations in Ecuador. Held in late June, this Andean festival honors the sun god *Inti*, an important figure in pre-Columbian cultures. The most notable celebrations take place in *Quito* and *Cuenca*, where indigenous communities perform traditional dances, music, and rituals. These celebrations are not just for tourists; they're an opportunity for Ecuadorians to reconnect with their heritage and share it with others.

Ecuadorians also have a rich history of religious festivals, often combining Catholic rituals with indigenous traditions. For instance, in the highlands, the *Fiesta de la Mama Negra* (The Black Mother Festival) is a colorful blend of Catholicism and indigenous beliefs. This festival, held in the town of *Latacunga* every November, features elaborate processions, traditional music, and dancing. It's a fascinating example of how Ecuadorians blend indigenous traditions with colonial influences, creating something uniquely Ecuadorian.

The importance of family cannot be overstated in Ecuadorian culture. Family gatherings, whether for a Sunday meal or a special celebration, are deeply cherished. It's common for extended families to come together, sharing food, stories, and laughter. If you're invited to someone's home, it's polite to bring a small gift, perhaps a bottle of wine or a box of chocolates. Ecuadorians are incredibly warm and welcoming, and a simple gesture of gratitude will be greatly appreciated.

What to Expect in Ecuadorian Hospitality

Ecuadorians are renowned for their hospitality, and travelers will often be struck by how welcoming and friendly the locals are. Whether you're visiting a remote village in the Andes or staying in a modern hotel in *Quito*, you'll experience a level of warmth and friendliness that makes Ecuador such a special place.

In the Andean highlands, it's common for locals to invite travelers to join them for a meal or share a drink. This is especially true in smaller villages, where residents often make a point of offering hospitality to visitors, regardless of whether they know them personally. One of the most heartfelt ways to connect with locals is by taking part in a traditional *pachamanca*, a community meal cooked in an earth oven. If you're lucky enough to be invited to one of these feasts, don't hesitate to accept—it's an opportunity to not only savor traditional foods but also engage in meaningful conversations with local families.

The *Ecuadorian sense of hospitality* extends to service in hotels and restaurants, where you'll often be treated like family. It's common for waiters, guides, and hotel staff to go out of their way to ensure you feel at home. Ecuadorians are genuinely proud of their country and eager to show visitors the best it has to offer. If you're in doubt or need help, don't hesitate to ask. Even in larger cities like *Quito* and *Guayaquil,* the locals will often take the time to offer you directions or give advice on places to visit.

One important thing to note is the pace of life in Ecuador. While major cities tend to be fast-paced, small towns and rural areas have a more relaxed rhythm. This means that things may take a bit longer than you're accustomed to. For instance, when you visit a local market or restaurant, it's not unusual for service to be slower, but that's simply part of the relaxed attitude toward life here. Patience and a smile go a long way.

Tipping and Bargaining in Ecuador

When it comes to tipping in Ecuador, the general rule is to leave about 10% in restaurants, although service charges are often already included in the bill, especially in tourist areas. It's always a good idea to check the bill to see if the service charge has been included. If not, a tip of 10% is customary, and it's often appreciated by staff.

In hotels, it's common to tip bellboys or housekeeping staff a few dollars for their service. If a guide takes you on a tour, consider tipping them a little extra, especially if they've gone above and beyond in providing you with an insightful experience.

Bargaining is a part of Ecuador's market culture, particularly in indigenous markets like the *Otavalo Market* and *Mercado Artesanal* in *Quito*. While the price on an item may be listed, it's often acceptable to haggle, especially if you're buying several items. However, don't be too aggressive. Ecuadorians are generally fair in their pricing, and if you're negotiating, it's always done with a sense of friendliness and respect. The key is to be polite, friendly, and not too forceful. Bargaining is seen as a way to build rapport, not as a confrontation.

In urban areas and supermarkets, bargaining is not the norm, and fixed prices are expected. But in more rural areas or local markets, haggling can be a fun part of the experience, so don't hesitate to give it a try. Just remember, the goal is not to get the lowest price but to engage in a friendly exchange with the vendor.

SUSTAINABLE TRAVEL IN ECUADOR

Ecuador, with its breathtaking natural landscapes and diverse ecosystems, offers travelers a rare opportunity to explore a country that is as rich in culture as it is in natural beauty. From the Amazon rainforest to the Galápagos Islands, and from the Andean highlands to the Pacific coast, Ecuador's environment is both fragile and invaluable. As a traveler, there's no better way to explore Ecuador than with a sustainable mindset—minimizing your environmental impact, supporting local communities, and giving back to the land that gives us so much.

In this chapter, I'll share insider tips on how to travel responsibly in Ecuador, with a focus on eco-friendly transportation, minimizing your environmental footprint, supporting local communities, and ways to give back while traveling. So, let's dive in and explore how you can experience this magnificent country while helping preserve its beauty for generations to come.

Eco-Friendly Transportation Options in Ecuador

When it comes to getting around Ecuador, the country offers several eco-friendly transportation options that allow you to reduce your carbon footprint while still making the most of your travel experience. From buses that connect major cities to alternatives like trains, bicycles, and electric cars, there are plenty of ways to explore the country without relying solely on fossil fuels.

In the larger cities, like Quito and Guayaquil, there has been an increased push for public transportation systems that help reduce congestion and emissions. The *Trolebus* system in Quito is a great example. This electric-powered bus system runs through key points of the city and is both affordable and environmentally friendly. For a more scenic route, consider taking the *Tren Crucero*, a luxurious train ride that runs from the highlands to the coast. The train itself has a minimal environmental impact, and the route takes you through some of Ecuador's most stunning landscapes, from the Andean foothills to the cloud forests.

For those who want to get more personal with the landscape, *bicycles* are becoming an increasingly popular and eco-conscious way to navigate through cities and rural areas. Many hostels, like *Bicycle Hostel* in Quito (located at *Calle Morales 123*, phone: +593 2 250 3539), offer bike rentals for exploring the city and nearby neighborhoods. You'll be able to weave through the cobblestone streets of historic Old Town Quito or venture out into the surrounding valleys, all while reducing your carbon footprint.

The Galápagos Islands, one of Ecuador's crown jewels, also offers environmentally friendly ways to explore its pristine shores. Several local tour operators are now promoting *eco-friendly boat tours* that focus on conservation and reducing the environmental impact on the archipelago. Tour companies like *Galápagos Eco Adventures* (phone: +593 5 252 0848) offer cruises and excursions that use sustainable practices, such as solar-powered vessels and low-impact activities.

Lastly, consider renting an *electric car* for road trips in the mainland. Companies such as *YAS Car Rental* (email: info@yasrentacar.com) offer electric vehicles that are perfect for those looking to reduce their carbon emissions. As electric car infrastructure continues to improve in Ecuador, this is becoming an increasingly viable option for eco-conscious travelers.

Responsible Tourism: How to Minimize Your Environmental Impact

As travelers, we have a responsibility to leave a minimal impact on the places we visit. Ecuador is home to some of the world's most biodiverse ecosystems, so it's crucial to travel in ways that respect both the environment and the local communities. Here are some key tips to minimize your environmental footprint while exploring Ecuador:

1. **Leave No Trace:** Whether you're hiking in the Andes, kayaking in the Amazon, or lounging on the beach, make sure to pack out everything you bring with you. Avoid leaving litter behind and dispose of your trash responsibly. This includes biodegradable items, as even they can take time to break down in certain environments.
2. **Use Reusable Items:** Say goodbye to plastic and opt for reusable water bottles, shopping bags, and containers. Many small towns and indigenous villages have local markets where you can refill your bottle, cutting down on single-use plastic.
3. **Respect Wildlife:** Ecuador is home to unique wildlife, particularly in the Galápagos and the Amazon, where animals are more sensitive to human presence. Always keep a respectful distance, avoid feeding animals, and follow local guidelines to ensure that your visit does not disturb the natural behavior of wildlife. This goes for both land and marine life.

4. **Support Sustainable Accommodation:** Look for hotels, hostels, and ecolodges that have earned certifications for sustainable practices. *Shandia Lodge* (located at *Km. 17, Tena* in the Amazon), for example, is a great eco-lodge that integrates sustainability into its operations. It uses renewable energy, offers organic meals, and works with the local community on conservation initiatives.
5. **Avoid Over-Tourism Areas:** In popular destinations like the Galápagos Islands, it's easy to fall into the trap of over-tourism. Try to visit during the off-peak seasons, book tours that focus on smaller groups, and support operators who emphasize environmental conservation.

Supporting Local Communities: How to Travel Responsibly

Ecuador's local communities—particularly indigenous populations—rely heavily on tourism for income, but it's important to make sure your visit benefits them directly and meaningfully. The most responsible way to do this is by supporting local businesses and artisans, participating in community-based tourism initiatives, and buying locally made products.

One of the best ways to support local communities is by staying in *community-run tourism initiatives*. For example, in the Amazon, the *Napo Wildlife Center* (located in the *Yasuni National Park*, phone: +593 2 281 5470) is an eco-lodge owned and operated by the local

Kichwa community. Visitors to the center help fund community projects such as education, healthcare, and conservation. By booking a stay here, you're directly supporting the preservation of the rainforest and the well-being of its inhabitants.

In the Andean highlands, towns like *Otavalo* and *Saquisilí* offer vibrant markets where artisans sell locally made goods such as handwoven textiles, pottery, and jewelry. These markets are not only a great place to shop for souvenirs but also an opportunity to support indigenous artisans directly. When buying, make sure to pay a fair price, and avoid purchasing mass-produced, imported goods that might undermine local businesses.

Volunteering and Giving Back While Traveling

One of the most meaningful ways to engage with Ecuador is by giving back through volunteering. Ecuador has many organizations that welcome travelers who want to contribute their time and skills in various fields, from environmental conservation to community development.

If you're passionate about wildlife conservation, consider volunteering with *The Galápagos Conservation Trust* (email: info@galapagosconservation.org.uk), which works on projects to preserve the delicate ecosystem of the islands. In the Amazon, *Amazon Conservation Team* (phone: +593 2 325 4106) has a range of volunteer opportunities, from environmental education to reforestation efforts.

For those interested in community development, organizations like *Fundación Natura* (phone: +593 2 292 0707) offer volunteer opportunities in areas like sustainable agriculture, health education, and local empowerment programs. Volunteering not only gives you the chance to make a positive impact but also allows you to engage deeply with the communities you visit.

PRACTICAL TIPS AND SAFETY

Traveling to Ecuador is a truly unforgettable experience, but as with any international destination, it's important to be prepared for the unexpected. This chapter will guide you through practical tips and essential safety advice to ensure your trip is not only thrilling but also smooth and secure. From staying connected to navigating local transportation, we'll cover everything you need to know so you can focus on exploring Ecuador's stunning landscapes and vibrant culture with peace of mind.

Travel Safety: Tips for a Smooth and Safe Experience in Ecuador

Ecuador is generally a safe destination for travelers, but like any country, it's important to stay aware of your surroundings and take common-sense precautions. Most visits to Ecuador are trouble-free, especially when you stick to well-trodden paths and follow some simple safety tips.

Stay aware of your belongings: Petty theft, particularly pickpocketing, can happen in busy areas such as markets, on public transport, and in larger cities like Quito and Guayaquil. Keep your valuables secure, preferably in a money belt or a zippered bag that you can wear close to your body. It's also a good idea to avoid flashing expensive jewelry, electronics, or large amounts of cash. If you're in a crowded area or on a bus, always keep an eye on your belongings.

Avoid walking alone at night: While Ecuador is home to friendly, welcoming people, it's always wise to be cautious when out and about after dark. Stick to well-lit, busy streets, especially in urban areas. If you're in cities like Quito or Guayaquil, try to arrange transport or a private ride when heading back to your accommodation late at night.

Use reputable transportation: Ecuador has a range of transportation options, but for safety and peace of mind, it's best to use trusted services. In larger cities, such as Quito, Guayaquil, and Cuenca, use established taxi services rather than hailing a cab off the street. Taxis from the airport or those ordered via phone are more reliable and generally safer. If you're ever in doubt, your hotel or guesthouse can help arrange trustworthy transportation.

Keep emergency numbers handy: It's always good to have local emergency numbers saved on your phone just in case. The emergency number for police in Ecuador is 101, while for medical emergencies, you should dial 171. For fires, call 102. Many hotels also provide their own emergency contacts for guest safety.

How to Stay Connected: Wi-Fi, SIM Cards, and Internet Access

Ecuador has a relatively well-developed telecommunications infrastructure, but it's important to plan ahead for staying connected during your trip.

Wi-Fi Access: Wi-Fi is readily available in most urban areas, and many hotels, cafes, and restaurants offer free Wi-Fi for their customers. In cities like Quito and Guayaquil, you'll have no trouble finding Wi-Fi, but in rural areas or remote locations, it can be less reliable. In these areas, you might need to rely on mobile data for internet access.

SIM Cards and Mobile Data: If you plan to use your phone to stay connected, the easiest option is to purchase a local SIM card. Ecuador's main mobile service providers are *Claro*, *Movistar*, and *Tuenti*. You can buy a SIM card at the airport, in shopping malls, or in small mobile stores in cities and towns. Prices are affordable, and many providers offer prepaid plans that include data, texts, and calls. It's a good idea to check if your phone is unlocked before you arrive, as locked phones may not work with local SIM cards.

For example, at *Claro* stores (located in most major cities like *Quito, Av. Amazonas y Naciones Unidas*), you can buy a SIM card for as little as $2 USD, and data plans typically range from $5 to $15 USD per month depending on the data allowance. If you're planning to stay connected for a while, the data packages provide good coverage and are a cost-effective way to stay online while exploring Ecuador.

Internet Cafes: Although Wi-Fi is common in urban areas, some rural towns or small villages may not have reliable internet. In these cases, internet cafes are a great option for getting online. Most towns have at least one internet cafe, where you can access email, browse the web, and make video calls.

Emergency Numbers and Healthcare Resources in Ecuador

While Ecuador is a safe destination for most travelers, it's always essential to be prepared for emergencies, especially when it comes to health-related matters.

Emergency Numbers: As mentioned, the emergency services number for police in Ecuador is 101, while for medical emergencies, you can dial 171. These services are available nationwide, and response times are generally prompt, especially in urban centers.

Healthcare Services: Ecuador offers both public and private healthcare services, with the quality of care varying depending on where you are. In major cities like Quito, Cuenca, and Guayaquil, you'll find well-equipped hospitals and clinics. Private hospitals generally offer a higher level of service and shorter wait times, though they can be more expensive.

For high-quality care, consider visiting *Hospital de la Mujer* in Quito (located at *Calle 10 de Agosto y Av. Mariana de Jesús*), a highly regarded hospital with modern facilities. It's always wise to have travel insurance that covers health emergencies while in Ecuador. For minor health concerns like cold symptoms or digestive issues, local pharmacies are well-stocked, and pharmacists often speak basic English.

If you need a dentist or medical specialist, it's a good idea to ask for recommendations from your hotel or fellow travelers. English-speaking doctors can be found in larger cities, and most major cities have 24-hour pharmacies available in case of urgent needs.

Navigating Ecuador's Transportation System: Buses, Taxis, and Ridesharing

Getting around Ecuador is relatively straightforward, but like any country, each mode of transport has its nuances. Here's a look at the most common options.

Buses: Ecuador's bus system is extensive, especially between major cities. Buses are the most affordable way to travel long distances within the country, with both local and intercity buses running regularly. The national bus terminal in Quito, called *Terminal Terrestre de Quitumbe* (located at *Av. Panamericana Sur*), is the main hub for long-distance travel to cities like Guayaquil, Cuenca, and Baños. A bus ride from Quito to Guayaquil takes about 8 hours and costs around $5–$10 USD. While buses are an inexpensive and reliable option, comfort levels can vary depending on the class of service.

When booking a bus, opt for *First Class* or *VIP* services for better comfort and air-conditioning, especially for longer trips. Most buses will have food and beverage options available during the journey. For shorter distances, such as between Quito and the nearby towns in the Andes, local buses are frequent and affordable. Keep in mind that buses can sometimes be crowded, so always keep a close eye on your belongings.

Taxis: Taxis are widely available in cities, and they are generally safe when ordered via a reputable service or through your hotel. In Quito, for example, you can call a taxi through the app *Easy Taxi* or ask your hotel to book one for you. A typical fare in Quito starts around $1.50 USD and can increase depending on the distance and time of day. Be sure to always take a registered taxi with a working meter to avoid disputes over fare.

Ridesharing: Ridesharing apps like *Uber* and *Cabify* are available in major cities like Quito and Guayaquil, offering a safe and convenient alternative to traditional taxis. These apps also allow you to see the estimated fare in advance, which can give you peace of mind about pricing.

Local Transport Options: In addition to taxis, cities like Quito and Cuenca have *Trolebus* and *Metro* systems that are inexpensive and efficient ways to navigate urban areas. In Quito, the *Trolebus* system runs on dedicated bus lanes and is electric, making it an eco-friendly option. Tickets for public transport in Quito cost about $0.25 USD per trip.

SHOPPING AND SOUVENIRS

Ecuador is a treasure trove of vibrant colors, rich textures, and unique craftsmanship, offering a vast array of shopping experiences that will leave you with lasting memories. From bustling markets to quaint artisan shops, the country is full of opportunities to find authentic handicrafts and meaningful souvenirs. But beyond the typical souvenirs, Ecuador offers a chance to bring home something truly special—items that reflect its diverse culture, its natural beauty, and the skills of its artisans. In this chapter, we'll explore the best places to shop for Ecuadorian handicrafts, what to buy, what to avoid, and how to make eco-friendly purchases that support both local communities and the environment.

Best Places to Shop for Authentic Ecuadorian Handicrafts

Ecuador is renowned for its high-quality artisan goods, and whether you're visiting the highlands, the Amazon rainforest, or the coastal region, you'll find vibrant markets brimming with beautiful, handcrafted products. But the charm of Ecuador's handicrafts is not just in their visual appeal; they are deeply rooted in the country's diverse indigenous cultures. Shopping for these treasures is more than just a retail experience; it's a way to connect with Ecuador's artistic heritage and its people.

Otavalo Market: If there's one place to experience Ecuador's traditional handicrafts, it's the *Plaza de los*

Ponchos in Otavalo. Located in the highland town of Otavalo, about two hours north of Quito, this market is famous for its colorful textiles, intricate handwoven ponchos, scarves, blankets, and bags. The indigenous Otavalan people are known for their expert weaving techniques, and the market is a showcase of their work. You'll also find hand-carved wood figurines, silver jewelry, and leather goods. The market is open every day, but the busiest day is Saturday when the plaza overflows with vendors and locals.

Address: *Plaza de los Ponchos, Otavalo, Imbabura*
Open: Monday–Saturday from 9:00 AM to 6:00 PM
Phone: +593 6-291-5320

Quito's La Ronda Street: In the heart of Quito's historic center, the cobblestone street of *La Ronda* is lined with artisan workshops, small galleries, and souvenir shops. Here, you can find beautifully handcrafted jewelry, hand-painted ceramics, intricate wood carvings, and copper crafts. The area also offers a glimpse into the traditional way of life, as many of the artisans still work in small studios behind their shops. La Ronda is also famous for its sweet treats, so take the time to sample local delicacies like *helados* (ice cream) and *torta de la riel* (sponge cake).

Address: *La Ronda, Quito*
Open: Monday–Saturday, 10:00 AM to 7:00 PM
Phone: +593 2-256-8363

Cuenca's Handicraft Shops: Cuenca, a charming colonial city in the southern highlands, is another hotspot for artisan goods. The city is famous for its *Panama hats* (which are actually made in Ecuador), as well as leather goods, ceramic pottery, and silver jewelry. You can wander through the narrow streets of Cuenca's historic center, visiting its small artisan shops. The *Mercado de Artesanías* (Craft Market) is a great place to find local pottery, leather bags, and intricate wood carvings. Cuenca's traditional handicrafts reflect both indigenous and Spanish influences, making for unique and meaningful souvenirs.

Address: *Mercado de Artesanías, Cuenca*
Open: Daily, 9:00 AM to 5:00 PM
Phone: +593 7-283-0102

Ecuadorian Markets: What to Buy and What to Avoid

Markets are a quintessential part of the Ecuadorian experience, and each one offers a different glimpse into the culture and the local lifestyle. However, not everything on display is worth your attention, and knowing what to buy and what to avoid will help you make more informed and meaningful purchases.

What to Buy:

1. **Handwoven Textiles:** Whether in Otavalo, Cuenca, or Quito, the handcrafted textiles are some of the finest items to purchase. These

include brightly colored ponchos, scarves, and shawls made from alpaca, sheep wool, or cotton. The vibrant colors and intricate patterns are a reflection of indigenous culture and are often woven by hand in small communities.
2. **Panama Hats:** Don't be fooled by the name— *Panama hats* originated in Ecuador. These finely woven straw hats are often made in the town of Montecristi, and they come in a range of styles and prices. The finest Panama hats are made from the *Toquilla* palm, and they are light, breathable, and durable—perfect for both practical use and as a stylish souvenir.
3. **Handcrafted Jewelry:** Ecuador is home to talented silversmiths, particularly in the cities of Cuenca and Quito. Look for beautiful silver jewelry pieces, often featuring local gemstones like emeralds, which are abundant in the country. You can find everything from delicate earrings to chunky statement necklaces.
4. **Wood and Leather Crafts:** Ecuador's artisans also excel in wood and leather craftsmanship. From carved wooden figurines and animal statues to hand-tooled leather bags and wallets, these items make for great, functional souvenirs. The leather is often dyed and molded into beautiful, intricate designs.

What to Avoid:

1. **Mass-Produced Souvenirs:** While many markets may sell mass-produced items, like

plastic trinkets or low-quality textiles, these do not reflect the true essence of Ecuador's artisanal heritage. Be mindful of products that seem overly cheap or identical from stall to stall—chances are they were made in factories and lack the authenticity and craftsmanship of true local art.
2. **Counterfeit 'Panama Hats':** Sadly, some cheaper imitations of the famous Panama hat are made from synthetic materials and are sold as genuine products. To ensure you're purchasing a real Panama hat, ask the vendor for information about the craftsmanship, and check if the hat is made from *Toquilla* straw. Quality Panama hats will often come with a certificate of authenticity, especially those made by master weavers.
3. **Animal Products:** Be cautious when purchasing souvenirs made from animal products, such as jewelry made from turtle shells or leather goods made from exotic animals. These products could be illegal, and purchasing them could contribute to the harm of local wildlife. Stick to ethically sourced products, and always ask about the origin of any animal-based items.

Eco-Friendly Souvenirs and Gifts to Bring Back Home

Ecuador is a country rich in natural beauty, and as travelers become more conscious of sustainability, eco-friendly souvenirs are an excellent way to support the environment while bringing home meaningful gifts.

Handmade Paper Goods: Many artisans in Ecuador craft paper products from recycled materials, such as banana leaves or old newspapers. These include journals, notebooks, and cards that make thoughtful gifts. By purchasing handmade paper goods, you're supporting artisans while reducing the demand for mass-produced paper.

Organic Coffee and Cocoa: Ecuador is a producer of world-class organic coffee and fine cocoa. Coffee lovers can find locally grown coffee beans in markets, often sold in burlap sacks, or packaged in eco-friendly bags. Ecuadorian chocolate, especially the fine dark chocolate made from local cacao beans, also makes for an irresistible souvenir. Many local chocolate shops in Quito and Cuenca offer chocolate made with sustainable farming practices.

Natural Beauty Products: Many eco-conscious brands in Ecuador produce skincare products using locally sourced ingredients, like Ecuadorian roses, cocoa butter, and indigenous herbs. These products are often organic, cruelty-free, and beautifully packaged, making them a great option for those looking to bring home natural wellness gifts.

Fair-Trade Crafts: Look for handicrafts that are part of the fair-trade movement. These items are often made by small cooperatives, ensuring that artisans are paid fairly for their work and that the environmental impact of production is minimized. You can find these items in specialized shops, such as *Kuna*, which has locations in both Quito and Cuenca.

DAY TRIPS AND OFF-THE-BEATEN-PATH ADVENTURES

Ecuador is a land of contrasts and surprises, and beyond the well-trodden tourist paths, the country offers a treasure trove of hidden gems and lesser-known spots that are perfect for those looking for adventure, culture, and breathtaking natural beauty. While cities like Quito, Guayaquil, and Cuenca are wonderful to explore, it's often the smaller towns, the quiet corners, and the off-the-beaten-path wonders that truly capture the essence of Ecuador. Whether you're seeking a tranquil escape in nature, a journey through indigenous communities, or an adrenaline-fueled adventure, Ecuador is waiting to show you its most captivating secrets. In this chapter, we'll dive into some of Ecuador's hidden gems and give you a taste of the authentic experiences that await just beyond the usual tourist destinations.

Exploring Ecuador's Hidden Gems: Secret Spots You Won't Want to Miss

Ecuador's charm lies in its diversity, and some of its most fascinating locations are tucked away from the typical tourist crowds. These hidden gems offer a glimpse of Ecuador's natural beauty, ancient traditions, and off-the-beaten-path wonders. To truly experience the essence of the country, take a detour from the popular routes and head towards places that remain unspoiled, quiet, and full of character.

Mindo Cloud Forest: Located just a two-hour drive from Quito, Mindo is a haven for nature lovers and bird watchers. This lush cloud forest, nestled in the Andes foothills, is teeming with life—over 500 species of birds, including the elusive toucan and the vibrant hummingbird, flutter through the canopy. Hiking through Mindo's misty trails, you'll discover waterfalls cascading down moss-covered rocks, rivers that sparkle in the sunlight, and rich flora that seems to pulse with the rhythm of the forest. There are also plenty of eco-lodges and small cafes where you can relax and enjoy the serene atmosphere. Mindo is a paradise for those looking to escape the hustle and bustle of city life, offering peaceful retreats and immersive nature experiences.

Address: *Mindo, Pichincha Province*
Open: *Daily, year-round*
Phone: +593 2-350-1065

Cajas National Park: If you're a fan of breathtaking mountain landscapes, Cajas National Park in the southern highlands of Ecuador is a must-see. Known for its misty paramo, high-altitude lakes, and wild beauty, Cajas is often overlooked by tourists heading to Cuenca. The park is an outdoor paradise, offering a network of trails that wind past glacial lakes, through dense forests, and across open tundra-like terrain. You may even spot llamas grazing peacefully by the lakeside or herds of wild horses. A hike in Cajas feels like stepping into another world, one that is rugged and wild, yet eerily peaceful. For an extra special experience, visit the park early in the morning when the mist still clings to the landscape, creating an ethereal atmosphere.

Address: *Cajas National Park, Azuay Province*
Open: Daily, 8:00 AM to 5:00 PM
Entry Fee: $2 per person
Phone: +593 7-288-1232

Day Trips from Quito: Adventure, Nature, and History

Quito, the capital city of Ecuador, is perfectly situated for day trips to explore the surrounding mountains, volcanoes, and picturesque towns. Whether you're an adrenaline junkie, a history buff, or a nature enthusiast, there's no shortage of places to explore within a few hours' drive from Quito.

Cotopaxi National Park: Just a short 1.5-hour drive south from Quito lies the majestic Cotopaxi National Park, home to one of the highest active volcanoes in the world. At 5,897 meters, Cotopaxi's snow-capped peak towers over the landscape, offering spectacular views and exciting adventures. Whether you're looking to hike to the base of the volcano, try mountain biking down its slopes, or simply take in the view from the comfort of a cozy lodge, Cotopaxi offers plenty of opportunities to connect with Ecuador's natural beauty. The park is also home to wildlife such as wild horses, deer, and Andean condors, making it a great spot for nature lovers.

Address: *Cotopaxi National Park, Cotopaxi Province*
Open: Daily, 8:00 AM to 4:00 PM
Entry Fee: $2–$5 per person
Phone: +593 3-280-4224

La Mitad del Mundo (Middle of the World): Located just outside Quito, La Mitad del Mundo is one of Ecuador's most famous landmarks. It marks the location of the Equator, where you can literally stand with one foot in the Northern Hemisphere and the other in the Southern Hemisphere. The monument itself is impressive, but the surrounding park also includes a museum dedicated to the history of the Equator and the science behind it. While it's a popular tourist stop, it's worth visiting to experience the unique feeling of being at the heart of the world. And, if you're looking for a more interactive experience, you can visit the nearby *Intiñan Museum*, which offers hands-on demonstrations of the effects of the Equator on physical phenomena.

Address: *La Mitad del Mundo, Pichincha Province*
Open: Daily, 9:00 AM to 5:00 PM
Entry Fee: $4 per person
Phone: +593 2-282-1397

Exploring the Quilotoa Loop: A Stunning Natural Circuit

If you're looking for an unforgettable adventure in Ecuador's Andean highlands, the Quilotoa Loop is an absolute must. This natural circuit connects several small towns, each one more charming and picturesque than the last, with the stunning Quilotoa Crater Lake as its crown jewel.

The loop, which is best explored over a few days, takes you through rural Ecuador, where the pace of life is slow, and the landscape is jaw-droppingly beautiful. Start your journey in the town of Latacunga, then travel south to explore villages like Sigchos, Zumbahua, and Chugchilán. Each town offers a different slice of Ecuadorian culture, from indigenous textiles and artisan crafts to lush valleys and Andean vistas. But the highlight of the trip is Quilotoa itself—a crater lake formed by a collapsed volcano that glows an otherworldly turquoise color. Whether you hike down to the lake's edge or simply take in the breathtaking view from the rim, Quilotoa is a place that will stay with you long after you've left.

Quilotoa Lake: The lake itself is part of the Quilotoa Volcano and offers some of the most stunning views in all of Ecuador. Hikers can descend to the lake's shore, but be prepared for the steep hike back up—at 3,900 meters above sea level, it can be a challenge. For those looking for something a bit less strenuous, there are various viewpoints around the rim where you can take in the dramatic landscape.

Address: *Quilotoa, Cotopaxi Province*
Open: Daily, 8:00 AM to 4:00 PM
Entry Fee: $2 per person
Phone: +593 3-281-5791

Discovering Ecuador's Indigenous Communities: Visits and Cultural Tours

Ecuador is home to a rich tapestry of indigenous cultures, each with its own traditions, language, and history. Visiting these communities not only offers you the chance to learn about their way of life, but also to support local economies in a meaningful way. These cultural tours provide an authentic, immersive experience that connects you with the heart of Ecuador's heritage.

The Saraguro People: Located in the southern highlands of Ecuador, the Saraguro community is known for its distinctive traditional dress and rich cultural practices. A visit to the town of Saraguro gives you the chance to meet artisans and watch traditional weaving techniques, or participate in cultural activities like weaving workshops or cooking classes. The Saraguro are welcoming and proud of their heritage, and a visit here offers an insight into their daily life that few tourists experience.

The Kichwa People of the Amazon: If you're traveling to the Amazon region, consider visiting one of the Kichwa communities near the town of Tena or Puyo. These indigenous people live in harmony with the rainforest and offer guided tours where you can learn about their sustainable way of life, medicinal plants, and spiritual practices. Tours typically include canoe rides through the jungle, visits to traditional homes, and cultural demonstrations.

Address: *Saraguro, Loja Province*
Phone: +593 7-273-5555

Visiting Ecuador's indigenous communities is an enriching experience that offers a deep connection to the country's history and culture. Always be respectful and seek permission before taking photographs, and remember that the best way to support these communities is by purchasing authentic crafts directly from artisans.

ECUADOR'S NIGHTLIFE AND ENTERTAINMENT

Ecuador is not just a land of stunning natural landscapes and rich history—it's also a country that knows how to have a good time when the sun sets. From the vibrant streets of Quito to the lively coastal towns, the nightlife and entertainment scene in Ecuador is as diverse as its culture. Whether you're a night owl looking for a chic bar, a music lover craving live performances, or a dancer ready to move to the rhythms of salsa and merengue, Ecuador offers a vibrant and exciting after-dark scene. In this chapter, we'll take you on a journey through Ecuador's best bars, clubs, and live music venues, explore the country's rich dance traditions, and highlight some of the biggest festivals and events that celebrate the heart and soul of Ecuadorian culture.

Quito's Best Bars, Clubs, and Live Music Venues

Quito, the capital city of Ecuador, is the heart of the country's nightlife scene, offering a range of options to suit all tastes. Whether you prefer a cozy cocktail bar, a high-energy nightclub, or a venue where you can listen to live music under the stars, Quito's nightlife has something to offer.

La Ronda: A Night in Old Quito

La Ronda is one of Quito's oldest and most charming neighborhoods, and it comes alive after dark. Strolling along its cobblestone streets, you'll find a variety of cozy bars and traditional taverns, each with its own character. These establishments serve up everything from craft cocktails to traditional Ecuadorian drinks like *canelazo*, a warm, spiced fruit punch often enjoyed during cooler nights.

The atmosphere here is relaxed and friendly, making it a perfect place to enjoy a drink while soaking up the historic surroundings. If you're lucky, you might even encounter street performers, musicians, or impromptu salsa sessions—La Ronda has a truly magical, old-world charm that draws both locals and tourists alike.

Contact: *La Ronda, Historic Center, Quito*
Open: Daily, 6:00 PM - 2:00 AM
Phone: +593 2-258-3471

Casa de Cerveza: A Craft Beer Haven

For beer lovers, Quito offers a growing craft beer scene, and one of the best spots to sample local brews is Casa de Cerveza. Located in the heart of the city, this bar offers an impressive selection of Ecuadorian craft beers, many of which are brewed right here in Quito. The laid-back atmosphere, complete with wooden tables and a friendly crowd, makes it a great spot to unwind after a day of sightseeing. The staff is always ready to recommend a beer that pairs perfectly with their tasty snacks.

Contact: *Casa de Cerveza, Plaza Foch, Quito*
Open: Daily, 4:00 PM - 12:00 AM
Phone: +593 2-255-9299

Bungalow 6: Dance the Night Away

If you're in the mood to dance, head to Bungalow 6 in Quito's lively *Plaza Foch* area. This trendy club is known for its eclectic mix of music, from Latin beats to electronic dance music, making it the perfect place to show off your dance moves. The ambiance is chic, with neon lights and a state-of-the-art sound system, but the real draw here is the dance floor, where locals and tourists alike come to party until the early hours of the morning.

Bungalow 6 often hosts themed nights and guest DJs, ensuring that every visit is a new and exciting experience. Whether you're a salsa enthusiast or just looking to have fun, Bungalow 6 offers an unforgettable night out in Quito.

Contact: *Bungalow 6, Plaza Foch, Quito*
Open: Thursday - Saturday, 9:00 PM - 3:00 AM
Phone: +593 2-254-2525

La Casa de la Música: Live Music with a View

For music lovers seeking an authentic experience, La Casa de la Música in Quito offers a blend of live performances and an incredible panoramic view of the city. Set on a hilltop, this venue hosts a variety of genres, including jazz, rock, and traditional Ecuadorian music. The venue's terrace is the perfect place to enjoy a cocktail while watching the sunset over the Andes, and the acoustics inside the venue are superb, making it a prime spot for intimate concerts.

Contact: *La Casa de la Música, Quito*
Open: Tuesday - Sunday, 6:00 PM - 12:00 AM
Phone: +593 2-250-2409

Salsa, Merengue, and Ecuadorian Dance Styles

No visit to Ecuador would be complete without diving into the country's vibrant dance scene. Ecuador's dance culture is a beautiful fusion of indigenous, African, and Spanish influences, and it pulses through the heart of the country's nightlife.

Salsa and Merengue: A Night of Rhythm

Salsa and merengue are the life of the party in many Ecuadorian nightclubs, especially in cities like Quito and

Guayaquil. The infectious beats of salsa get everyone on their feet, and whether you're an experienced dancer or a beginner, you'll find plenty of places to learn, practice, and have fun.

Quito's *La Bodeguita de los Comediantes* is one of the most popular spots for salsa enthusiasts. Every night, locals and visitors pack the dance floor, twirling and spinning to the sounds of live salsa bands. The energetic vibe and the joy of dancing make it an unforgettable experience. Another great spot for dancing is *Salsa Vibe* in the *Plaza Foch* area, where you'll find a mix of salsa, bachata, and reggaeton.

Bachata: A Slow Dance with Passion

Bachata, a slower and sensual dance style from the Dominican Republic, is also hugely popular in Ecuador. Clubs like *La Bodeguita* and *Bungalow 6* often feature bachata nights, where the intimate rhythms create a romantic atmosphere. If you're looking to learn, many salsa clubs offer bachata lessons in addition to salsa, making it easy for anyone to dive into the dance scene.

Indigenous Dance Styles

In addition to Latin rhythms, Ecuador is also home to a variety of indigenous dance styles that are a key part of the country's cultural identity. Traditional dances like the *Inti Raymi* (celebrating the sun god) or the *Diablada* (devil dance) can be witnessed at local festivals, where dancers wear elaborate costumes and perform to live music. These dances are deeply rooted in Ecuador's history and are a stunning display of the country's indigenous heritage.

Festivals and Events: Celebrating Ecuador's Rich Cultural Heritage

Ecuador's festivals are an explosion of color, music, and joy, reflecting the country's diverse cultural heritage. These celebrations, which take place throughout the year, give you an authentic taste of Ecuadorian life and are the perfect way to immerse yourself in the local culture.

Carnival in Guaranda

If you're in Ecuador during Carnival season, don't miss the vibrant celebrations in Guaranda, a small town in the Sierra region. Known as one of the best Carnival festivals in the country, the event is a raucous mix of parades, street parties, traditional dances, and plenty of music. The streets are filled with people dressed in colorful costumes, throwing water balloons and paint, creating an atmosphere of pure revelry.

Contact: *Guaranda, Bolívar Province When: February or March (dates vary)*

Fiestas de la Mama Negra in Latacunga

One of the most unique cultural events in Ecuador is the *Fiestas de la Mama Negra* in Latacunga. Celebrated every November, this festival honors the indigenous Virgin of the Candelaria. The event features a blend of indigenous and Spanish traditions, including a parade with vibrant costumes, religious processions, and the crowning of the *Mama Negra*, a person chosen to represent the Virgin. Expect fireworks, traditional music, and plenty of food as you immerse yourself in this captivating celebration of Ecuador's cultural diversity.

Contact: *Latacunga, Cotopaxi Province*
When: November (dates vary)

The Quito Festival: Music and Dance in the Capital

Quito's *Fiestas de Quito* is a month-long celebration in December, marking the founding of the city. The event is a city-wide party, with street parades, live music performances, and traditional dances. The highlight is the *Chiva Party*, where revelers hop on colorful buses (known as *chivas*) and cruise through the city while singing and dancing to traditional music. If you're in Quito during this time, be sure to take part in the festivities for a truly local experience.

Contact: *Quito, Pichincha Province*
When: December 6-24

ITINERARIES FOR DIFFERENT TYPES OF TRAVELERS

Ecuador is a land of extraordinary diversity, offering something for every type of traveler. Whether you're here for cultural immersion, thrilling adventures, family bonding, or eco-conscious exploration, the country has a perfect itinerary waiting for you. In this chapter, we'll dive into tailored travel routes that will help you explore the best Ecuador has to offer in a way that suits your interests and passions. From the high-altitude peaks of the Andes to the tropical rainforests of the Amazon, Ecuador promises a journey of unforgettable experiences. So, pack your bags and let's embark on these unique journeys through one of the most biodiverse countries on the planet.

The Classic Ecuador Itinerary: 7 Days to See the Highlights

If you're short on time but want to experience the essence of Ecuador, this 7-day itinerary is the perfect introduction. It's designed for travelers who want to see the highlights: the colonial charm of Quito, the natural beauty of the Andes, the wildlife of the Galápagos Islands, and the allure of Ecuador's lush cloud forests.

Day 1-2: Quito – The Historic Capital

Start your journey in Quito, Ecuador's capital, nestled high in the Andes at 2,850 meters (9,350 feet). Quito is a UNESCO World Heritage Site known for its well-preserved colonial architecture. Spend your first day wandering through the historic center, where cobblestone streets and grand churches like *La Compañía de Jesús* take you back to Ecuador's colonial past. Don't miss a visit to the *Panecillo Hill*, where you can enjoy panoramic views of the city framed by the majestic Cotopaxi volcano.

On day 2, take a trip to the *Middle of the World*, located just 30 minutes north of Quito. The *Mitad del Mundo* monument marks the equator line, and you can stand with one foot in each hemisphere.

Contact: *Quito Tourist Information Center*
Location: *Plaza de la Independencia, Quito*
Open: 9:00 AM - 6:00 PM
Phone: +593 2-299-2323

Day 3-4: Cotopaxi National Park – Andes Adventures

Head south from Quito to the striking *Cotopaxi National Park*. The park is home to the active *Cotopaxi Volcano*, one of the highest active volcanoes in the world. For adventurous travelers, a hike or even a trek to the *Refugio José Ribas* at 4,800 meters (15,748 feet) offers spectacular views and the chance to see the snow-capped peak up close.

For those not quite ready to tackle the volcano's slopes, the park offers plenty of wildlife watching, such as spotting wild horses, llamas, and the Andean condor. In the evening, you can relax in one of the charming lodges nearby, like the *Tambopaxi Lodge*, which offers a cozy respite with stunning views of the Cotopaxi peak.

Contact: *Cotopaxi National Park Visitor Center Location*: *Cotopaxi Province, Ecuador Open*: Daily, 8:00 AM - 4:00 PM *Phone*: +593 2-227-8987

Day 5-6: The Galápagos Islands – Wildlife Wonderland

No trip to Ecuador would be complete without visiting the world-renowned Galápagos Islands. Catch a flight from Quito to *Baltra Island*, where you'll begin your island-hopping adventure. The Galápagos are a nature lover's paradise, with endemic species such as the famous giant tortoises, marine iguanas, and the iconic blue-footed booby.

You can explore by boat, taking guided excursions to *Santa Cruz*, *Isabela*, and *San Cristóbal* islands. Activities include snorkeling with sea lions, diving with hammerhead sharks, or simply walking along the shores of volcanic landscapes. The Galápagos National Park offers visitors the opportunity to discover the beauty of nature with sustainable, guided tours.

Contact: *Galápagos National Park Directorate*
Location: *Puerto Ayora, Santa Cruz Island*
Open: *Daily, 8:00 AM - 6:00 PM*
Phone: *+593 5-252-6500*

Day 7: Return to Quito

Finish your trip by flying back to Quito, perhaps catching a cultural show or visiting one of the many art galleries before heading to the airport. You've now experienced the iconic highlights of Ecuador!

Ecuador for Adventure Seekers: 10-Day Itinerary of Thrills and Nature

For those craving adventure, Ecuador is a playground of thrilling activities. From hiking through high-altitude landscapes to exploring remote jungles and surfing pristine beaches, this 10-day itinerary is packed with adrenaline-pumping fun and natural beauty.

Day 1-2: Banos – Waterfalls and Adventure Sports

Kick off your adventure in the town of *Baños*, known as the adventure capital of Ecuador. Located at the base of the Tungurahua volcano, Baños offers thrilling activities like white-water rafting, canyoning, and bungee jumping off the *San Francisco Bridge*. Spend your first day exploring the town's beautiful waterfalls, including *Pailón del Diablo* (Devil's Cauldron), a waterfall that plunges into a mist-filled gorge.

On Day 2, take a dip in the natural hot springs or join a guided bike ride along the *Ruta de las Cascadas*, a scenic route that passes numerous waterfalls. If you're feeling daring, try paragliding over the stunning valley for an aerial view of Baños.

Contact: *Baños Adventure Tours Location*: *Baños de Agua Santa, Tungurahua Province Phone*: +593 3-274-1211

Day 3-4: Quilotoa Loop – High-altitude Hiking and Culture

Next, make your way to the *Quilotoa Loop*, a scenic route that takes you through rural Andean villages, stunning mountain landscapes, and the breathtaking *Quilotoa Crater Lake*. This emerald-green lake, set in the caldera of an ancient volcano, offers some of the most stunning views in Ecuador. Hike down to the lake's shore or just soak in the view from the rim. The area is also home to traditional indigenous communities, and you can learn about their culture as you trek through local villages like *Zumbahua* and *Chugchilán*.

Day 5-6: Tena – Amazon Rainforest Adventures

For the next leg of your journey, head to the *Amazon Basin* town of *Tena*. Here, you can immerse yourself in the Amazon rainforest by staying in eco-lodges, such as the *Napo Wildlife Center*. Enjoy canoe rides along the *Napo River*, visit indigenous communities, and explore lush jungle trails with local guides who are experts in spotting wildlife like monkeys, birds, and reptiles.

Contact: *Napo Wildlife Center Lodge*
Location: *Tena, Napo Province*
Phone: +593 2-229-0600

Day 7-8: Mindo – Cloud Forest Adventures

For a change of pace, head to *Mindo*, a town set in the Ecuadorian cloud forest. This region is perfect for nature lovers, with activities like birdwatching, zip-lining through the forest canopy, and hiking to hidden waterfalls. Mindo is also a paradise for butterfly enthusiasts, and you'll find numerous butterfly farms where you can see vibrant species up close.

Contact: *Mindo Cloud Forest Tour Operators*
Location: *Mindo, Pichincha Province*
Phone: +593 2-286-1204

Day 9-10: Montañita – Surf and Beach Vibes

End your adventure in the laid-back beach town of *Montañita* on Ecuador's Pacific coast. Known for its great surf and bohemian vibe, Montañita offers the perfect place to unwind after your action-packed journey. Whether you're surfing the waves or lounging on the beach, this vibrant beach town is a great place to relax and reflect on your adventurous trip.

Contact: *Montañita Surf Schools*
Location: *Montañita, Santa Elena Province*
Phone: +593 4-258-8503

Family-Friendly Ecuador: 7 Days for All Ages

Traveling with children or family members of all ages? Ecuador is an excellent destination for families, offering a mix of adventure, nature, and culture that will entertain and engage everyone. This 7-day itinerary takes you from the Andes to the Amazon, with plenty of opportunities for family-friendly fun.

Day 1-2: Quito – Culture and Fun for All Ages

Start in Quito with a visit to the *Yaku Water Museum* and the *Museo Templo del Sol*, where kids can learn about the country's history in a hands-on, interactive way. Then, take a ride on the *Teleférico* (cable car) to the top of *Pichincha Volcano* for stunning views of the city.

Day 3-4: Cotopaxi National Park – Wildlife Watching

Explore Cotopaxi National Park with a family-friendly hike or a visit to the *Cotopaxi Interpretation Center*, where kids can learn about the park's geology and wildlife. You might even spot wild horses and llamas.

Day 5-6: Amazon Rainforest – Nature Adventures

Travel to the Amazon and stay in family-friendly eco-lodges like the *Sacha Lodge*, where families can explore the jungle together. Take a boat ride along the river, spot monkeys, and enjoy wildlife tours tailored

for younger audiences.

Day 7: Return to Quito

Wrap up your trip with a final day in Quito, visiting the *La Carolina Park* for some relaxation before heading home.

CONCLUSION
Final Thoughts on Ecuador: Why It's the Perfect Destination for Your Next Adventure

Ecuador is a country that constantly surprises, delights, and leaves travelers with a sense of wonder. Whether you find yourself wandering through the cobblestone streets of Quito, taking in the towering peaks of the Andes, or immersing yourself in the diverse ecosystems of the Amazon rainforest, there's no question that Ecuador offers a unique and unforgettable experience.

What makes Ecuador stand out as a travel destination is its incredible diversity, all packed into a small but mighty land. You can start your day with a hearty breakfast in the high-altitude city of Quito, then take a short flight to the Galápagos Islands and be swimming with sea lions in the afternoon. The next day, find yourself riding horses across the Andean páramo, or ziplining through the misty cloud forests of Mindo. From the snowy peaks of the mountains to the humid heat of the jungle, Ecuador offers a microcosm of everything a traveler could wish for.

The charm of Ecuador lies not only in its diverse geography but also in its welcoming people. Ecuadorians are some of the warmest and most gracious hosts you'll find anywhere in the world. Their deep pride in their culture, traditions, and natural heritage is palpable, and they are eager to share it with visitors. Whether it's joining a local festival, tasting the freshest ceviche, or learning about centuries-old indigenous traditions, the connection you'll form with the people of Ecuador is part of the magic that makes the country so special.

Another standout feature of Ecuador is its affordability. While some destinations in South America may require a hefty budget, Ecuador offers a more accessible experience without sacrificing quality. Hotels, restaurants, and transportation are reasonably priced, making it possible to experience all the country has to offer, even on a modest budget.

For adventure seekers, Ecuador is truly a paradise. From the slopes of Cotopaxi to the surf breaks of Montañita, there's no shortage of adrenaline-pumping activities to keep you on your toes. Nature lovers will find endless opportunities for hiking, wildlife watching, and photography in some of the world's most biodiverse environments. For history buffs, Ecuador's rich cultural heritage, from ancient Incan ruins to colonial architecture, provides a deep sense of connection to the past.

But perhaps what makes Ecuador truly unforgettable is its commitment to sustainable tourism. From eco-lodges in the Amazon to conservation programs in the Galápagos, the country is working hard to protect its natural wonders while offering responsible travel experiences. As travelers, we have a unique opportunity to be part of this movement by supporting the local businesses, guides, and communities that make it all possible.

In short, Ecuador is not just a place you visit; it's a place you experience. It invites you to discover new landscapes, tastes, and ways of life, all while creating memories that will stay with you long after you've left. Whether you're seeking adventure, culture, relaxation, or a combination of all three, Ecuador has everything you need to make your next adventure one for the books.

Additional Resources: Websites, Blogs, and Travel Forums for More Info

Ecuador is a country that is constantly evolving, with new experiences and destinations to explore. To stay updated on the latest travel tips, insights, and recommendations, here are some valuable resources:

1. **Ecuador Tourism Board** – The official tourism website offers comprehensive information on destinations, events, and travel tips across the country.
   - Website: www.ecuador.travel
2. **Lonely Planet's Ecuador Travel Guide** – A trusted resource for travelers, this guide offers detailed information on destinations, accommodation, and activities.
   - Website: www.lonelyplanet.com/ecuador
3. **GringoTree** – A popular blog and forum for expats and travelers, GringoTree provides tips on everything from cultural events to practical advice on navigating life in Ecuador.
   - Website: www.gringotree.com
4. **Ecuadorian Travel Forum (TripAdvisor)** – This community-driven forum is filled with personal travel stories, recommendations, and tips from people who have been there and done that.
   - Website: www.tripadvisor.com
5. **The Galápagos Conservation Trust** – If you're planning to visit the Galápagos, this is a great resource to learn about the islands' conservation efforts and sustainable tourism practices.
   - Website: www.gct.org
6. **Ecuadorian Amazon Travel** – For those looking to explore the Amazon basin, this website is full of detailed itineraries, eco-lodges, and wildlife excursions.
   - Website: www.ecuadorianamazon.com

Stay Connected: How to Keep Up with Ecuadorian Travel Trends

Travel trends in Ecuador are constantly changing, as the country continues to evolve as a top destination for adventure, culture, and eco-tourism. Staying connected to the latest developments will ensure that your trip is filled with the most up-to-date information and experiences. Here's how to stay in the loop:

1. **Follow Social Media Accounts** – Social media is a great way to stay informed about current events, festivals, and special promotions. Follow local tourism boards, travel bloggers, and tour operators on Instagram, Facebook, and Twitter. Look for hashtags like #EcuadorTravel, #GalapagosIslands, or #VisitEcuador to see what's happening in real-time.
2. **Subscribe to Newsletters** – Many local tour companies, eco-lodges, and even the Ecuadorian Ministry of Tourism offer newsletters that highlight new destinations, seasonal activities, and updates on sustainable travel efforts. Subscribing to these newsletters will help you stay ahead of the curve when planning your trip.
3. **Join Online Travel Communities** – Online forums such as *Reddit* (specifically the /r/Ecuador subreddit) and *Ecuador Travel* Facebook groups are great for connecting with other travelers and locals. You'll find firsthand

accounts, insider tips, and even recommendations for off-the-beaten-path adventures.
4. **Keep an Eye on Sustainable Travel Initiatives** – Ecuador is at the forefront of eco-tourism in South America, and there are always new initiatives being launched to protect its natural environments. To make sure you're supporting responsible tourism practices, check out organizations like *Ecuador's Ministry of Tourism* or *Galápagos Conservancy* for the latest sustainability efforts and eco-friendly travel options.
5. **Travel Apps** – Apps like *Maps.me*, *Google Maps*, and *TripIt* are invaluable for navigating Ecuador's diverse landscapes. There are also specialized apps for activities like hiking, birdwatching, and wildlife photography, which can help you make the most of your time in nature.

APPENDICES

A. Useful Spanish Phrases for Travelers

While many Ecuadorians working in tourism speak English, especially in larger cities and more frequented tourist areas, speaking some Spanish will enhance your travel experience and deepen your connection with locals. Ecuador is a country rich in culture and history, and knowing a few key phrases can make all the difference, whether you're navigating the bustling markets of Quito, negotiating a fare with a taxi driver, or striking up a conversation with a friendly local in a remote village.

Here's a quick guide to some essential phrases and words that will help you get by in Ecuador:

Basic Greetings:

- **Hola** (OH-lah) – Hello
- **Buenos días** (BWEH-nohs DEE-ahs) – Good morning
- **Buenas tardes** (BWEH-nahs TAR-dess) – Good afternoon
- **Buenas noches** (BWEH-nahs NOH-chess) – Good evening / Good night
- **¿Cómo estás?** (KOH-moh eh-STAHSS?) – How are you?
- **Bien, gracias. ¿Y tú?** (BYEHN, GRAH-syahs. EE TOO?) – Fine, thank you. And you?
- **Mucho gusto** (MOO-choh GOO-stoh) – Nice to meet you

Useful Questions:

- **¿Dónde está...?** (DOHN-deh es-TAH) – Where is...?
- **¿Cuánto cuesta?** (KWAN-toh KWEH-stah) – How much does it cost?
- **¿A qué hora?** (AH keh OH-rah) – At what time?
- **¿Habla inglés?** (AH-blah een-GLEHS) – Do you speak English?
- **¿Puedo pagar con tarjeta de crédito?** (PWEH-doh pah-GAHR kohn tar-HEH-tah deh KREH-dee-toh?) – Can I pay with a credit card?

- ¿Me puede ayudar? (MEH PWEH-deh ah-yoo-DAHR?) – Can you help me?

Emergency and Help:

- ¡Ayuda! (AH-yoo-dah) – Help!
- ¿Dónde está el hospital? (DOHN-deh es-TAH el oh-spee-TAHL?) – Where is the hospital?
- **Necesito un médico.** (NEH-seh-SEE-toh oon MEH-dee-koh) – I need a doctor.
- ¿Tiene un teléfono? (TEE-eh-neh oon teh-LEH-foh-noh?) – Do you have a phone?

Dining and Shopping:

- **La cuenta, por favor.** (LA KWEHN-tah, por fah-VOHR) – The bill, please.
- ¿Tienen platos vegetarianos? (TEE-eh-nen PLAH-tohs veh-heh-TAH-ree-ah-nohs?) – Do you have vegetarian dishes?
- ¿Cuánto cuesta esto? (KWAN-toh KWEH-stah ES-toh?) – How much is this?
- ¡Está delicioso! (EH-stah deh-lee-SYOH-soh) – It's delicious!

Mastering these phrases will help you navigate Ecuador with ease and will likely earn you a smile from locals who appreciate any effort to speak their language.

B. Directory of Tour Operators, Travel Agencies, and Guides

Ecuador is a diverse and complex country, and one of the best ways to explore its varied landscapes, wildlife, and culture is with the help of local experts. Below is a list of trusted tour operators, agencies, and guides who can help you craft the perfect itinerary, from trekking in the Andes to exploring the Galápagos Islands.

Galápagos Islands:

- **Galápagos Travel**
  Specializing in tours and cruises around the Galápagos Archipelago, Galápagos Travel offers everything from day trips to multi-day expeditions. Their guides are naturalists who provide in-depth knowledge of the unique ecosystem of the islands.
  - **Website:** www.galapagos.travel
  - **Phone:** +593 5 252 6316
  - **Email:** info@galapagos.travel

Andes and Amazon Adventures:

- **Shamrock Adventures**
  Shamrock specializes in high-altitude treks and multi-day hiking expeditions in the Andes, including visits to indigenous communities and eco-lodges in the Amazon. They offer tailored experiences for all levels of adventurers.
  - **Website:** www.shamrockadventures.com
  - **Phone:** +593 98 726 5171

- Email: info@shamrockadventures.com

Quito City Tours:

- **Andes Ecotours**
  This eco-friendly tour operator focuses on responsible travel in Quito and the surrounding areas, offering walking tours of the city's historical center, visits to museums, and hikes in nearby national parks.
    - Website: www.andesecotours.com
    - Phone: +593 2 228 6073
    - Email: info@andesecotours.com

General Travel Agencies:

- **Viajar Ecuador**
  Offering comprehensive travel services, Viajar Ecuador provides both group and custom tours throughout the country. Their services range from city tours and adventure treks to cultural excursions.
    - Website: www.viajarescuador.com
    - Phone: +593 2 222 6981
    - Email: info@viajarescuador.com

C. Travel Resources: Websites and Apps to Make Your Trip Easier

To enhance your travel experience in Ecuador, here are some helpful websites and mobile apps that can assist with everything from itinerary planning to currency conversion.

Websites:

1. **Ecuador Travel**
   The official tourism website of Ecuador is a fantastic resource for up-to-date information on destinations, events, festivals, and practical tips for visitors.
   - Website: www.ecuador.travel
2. **TripAdvisor**
   TripAdvisor provides reviews, ratings, and recommendations for hotels, restaurants, activities, and attractions throughout Ecuador. A great tool for checking out what other travelers are saying.
   - Website: www.tripadvisor.com
3. **Ecuadorian Amazon**
   If you're interested in exploring the Amazon basin, this site offers comprehensive details about eco-lodges, tours, and wildlife excursions.
   - Website: www.ecuadorianamazon.com

Apps:

1. **Maps.me**
   A must-have for navigating Ecuador's diverse landscapes. This app allows you to download offline maps, so you won't have to worry about getting lost in the remote areas of the country.
   - Available for iOS and Android.

2. **XE Currency Converter**
   Ecuador uses the U.S. dollar, but XE Currency is a handy tool to keep track of exchange rates, especially when withdrawing cash from ATMs or making larger purchases.
   - Available for iOS and Android.
3. **Buses Ecuador**
   For traveling around the country by bus, this app provides schedules, routes, and booking options, making intercity travel more convenient.
   - Available for iOS and Android.

D. Ecuador's Public Holidays and How They Affect Travel Plans

Ecuador celebrates a number of national holidays throughout the year, and these days can affect local business hours, transportation, and tourist attractions. During public holidays, many shops and offices close, and public transport may be limited or overcrowded, especially during festivals. However, holidays are also an excellent opportunity to experience Ecuador's vibrant culture, with lively festivals, parades, and local celebrations happening across the country.

Here's a quick overview of some important public holidays in Ecuador:

- **Carnival (February/March)** – Celebrated nationwide with parades, music, and festivities. If you're in

coastal cities like Guayaquil or in the highlands around Cuenca, expect street parties and festivals.
- **Ecuadorian Independence Day (August 10)** – A national holiday marking Ecuador's independence from Spain. Expect grand parades in cities like Quito, with plenty of patriotic displays and local performances.
- **Day of the Dead (November 2)** – While this is a solemn holiday, it's also a time for visiting cemeteries and honoring ancestors. It's particularly important in the Andean regions.
- **Christmas (December 25)** – A major holiday, often spent with family. Many shops close for a few days, and public transport can be limited.
- **New Year's Eve (December 31)** – A time for grand celebrations, especially in Quito, where you'll see burning effigies, fireworks, and street parties that last well into the night.

Make sure to plan accordingly, as some attractions may be closed or crowded during these holidays, but it's also a fantastic opportunity to experience the local culture firsthand.

Thank you so much for joining me on this journey through "Ecuador Travel Guide: Experience the Vibrant Culture and Breath-taking Landscapes"

I hope this book has inspired and informed you, and that you've found it as enjoyable to read as it was for me to write.

If you found the content helpful, I would be incredibly grateful if you could take a moment to leave a review on Amazon. Your feedback not only helps me improve but also assists other readers in discovering this book. Reviews are a vital part of the process, and your support means the world to me.

To leave a review, simply visit the book's page on Amazon and share your thoughts. Whether it's a few words or a detailed review, every bit of feedback is appreciated.

Thank you again for your support, and happy reading!

Warm regards,

Aiden C. Brooks

Made in the USA
Columbia, SC
17 June 2025